Klett

10-Minuten-Training

Englisch Grammatik

Direct Speech – Indirect Speech

Reported Speech

7./8. Klasse

Kleine Lernportionen für jeden Tag

Petra Lihocky, Götz Maier-Dörner

Klett Lerntraining

Autoren:
Petra Lihocky
Kapitel 1: Aufgabe 3; Kapitel 2: Aufgabe 7, 8, 11; Kapitel 3: Aufgabe 1, 2;
Kapitel 5: Aufgabe 5, 6, 7, 8, 9; Kapitel 6: Aufgabe 3, 4

Götz Maier-Dörner
Kapitel 2: Aufgabe 6; Kapitel 3: Aufgabe 4; Kapitel 5: Aufgabe 4; Kapitel 6: Aufgabe 5;
Kapitel 8: Aufgabe 1, 6, 7, 8, 9

Bibliografische Information der Deutschen Nationalbibliothek
Die Deutsche Nationalbibliothek verzeichnet diese Publikation in der
Deutschen Nationalbibliografie; detaillierte bibliografische Daten sind
im Internet über http://dnb.dnb.de abrufbar.

2. Auflage 2018

www.klett-lerntraining.de

Zeichnungen S. 54: Katja Rau, Berglen
Umschlaggestaltung: Sabine Kaufmann, Stuttgart
Umschlagfoto: www.thomas-weccard.de
Layout und Satz: tebitron gmbh, Gerlingen
Druck: medienhaus Plump gmbH, Rheinbreitbach
Printed in Germany
ISBN 978-3-12-927519-1

Inhaltsverzeichnis

Vorwort

Hallo!

Wie ist das bei dir? Blickst du bei der direkten und indirekten Rede im Englischen auch oft nicht so richtig durch? Und du weißt gar nicht, wie du üben sollst?

Keine Sorge, die Verwendung von direkter und indirekter Rede kannst du in diesem Buch super üben.

Unser Tipp: Lerne nicht alles an einem Tag. Übe lieber jeden Tag **10 Minuten**! Das geht superschnell und du übst trotzdem intensiver als sonst.

1 In diesem Heft findest du viele Übungen, mit denen du die indirekte Rede im Englischen trainieren kannst.

Die kleine Stoppuhr erinnert dich daran: besser kleine Lernportionen!

Tipp Hier bekommst du wichtige Tipps zu den Übungen.

★☆ Leichtere Übungen haben einen Stern ★☆ und etwas schwerere Übungen haben zwei Sterne ★★. Beginne am besten mit den leichteren!

Lösungen Hinten im Buch findest du die Lösungen zu den Übungen.

Wir wünschen dir viel Erfolg!

Deine Klett Lerntraining Redaktion

Immer nur 10 Minuten!

1 Direct Speech and Indirect Speech – Einleitendes Verb im *present tense*

Tipp

Mit der direkten Rede gibst du wieder, was jemand sagt oder denkt. Das, was gesagt oder gedacht wird, wird dabei in Anführungszeichen gesetzt. Steht der Einleitungssatz am Ende, setzt du, anders als im Deutschen, ein Komma vor die Anführungszeichen.

"I like this movie very much," says Annie.
Carl answers: "I don't like it, it is boring."
Annie asks: "How about you, mom? Do you like it?"

Bitte Lesen

1 ★☆ **Ergänze, was Familie Brown erzählt. Benutze die direkte Rede und denke an die Anführungszeichen.**

I'm tired.

„I'm tired" says Carl.

Didn't you sleep well?

Mrs Brown answers: "Didn't you sleep well?"

I have read such an exciting book yesterday, so I went to bed late last night.

Carl explains: "I read such an exciting book yesterday so I went to bed late last night."

Well, you shouldn't read that much this evening. Otherwise you'll be tired tomorrow, too.

Mrs Brown tells him: "Well, you shouldn't read that much this evening. Otherwise your'll be tired tomorrow, too."

1 Direkt Speech and Indirect Speech – Einleitendes Verb im *present tense*

Tipp

Die indirekte Rede gebrauchst du, genau wie im Deutschen, wenn du wiedergeben willst, was jemand gesagt hat.

Die indirekte Rede besteht immer aus einem Einleitungssatz und einem Folgesatz, dazwischen steht kein Komma.

Wenn du am selben Tag davon berichtest, steht das einleitende Verb im *present tense*. Du übernimmst die Zeitformen und Zeitangaben der direkten Rede unverändert in die indirekten Rede.

Annie says: "The weather is fine." → *She says that the weather is fine.*

2 ★☆ **Annie telefoniert mit ihrer Tante. Ihre Mutter möchte mithören, aber der Lautsprecher funktioniert nicht. Gib in indirekter Rede wieder, was Annies Tante erzählt.**

Aunt Susan says:

"I am in Edinburgh right now." "It's an amazing town."

"There are lots of wonderful ancient buildings."

"I have to visit the castle this afternoon."

"I like the town."

a) *Aunt Susan says that she is in Edinburgh right now.*

b) She tells me ______

c) She thinks ______

d) She mentions ______

e) She says ______

Tipp

Für den einleitenden Satz benutzt du Verben des Sagens und Denkens, z. B. *say, think, hope, explain, tell sb., mention, promise.* Oder auch *write*, wenn es um etwas Geschriebenes geht.

Die indirekte Rede im Folgesatz wird mit *that* angeschlossen. Du kannst das *that* aber auch weglassen.

Tipp

Denke daran, die Personalpronomen in der indirekten Rede anzupassen! *I* wird z. B. zu *she* oder *he*. Du musst auch darauf achten, die Verbform anzupassen!

She says: "I like Edinburgh." → *She says she likes Edinburgh.*

3 ★★ **In Carls Klasse sind heute deutsche Austauschschüler zu Gast. Einer von ihnen, Benjamin, stellt sich vor. Gib seine Aussagen in indirekter Rede wieder. Suche dir dazu jeweils ein einleitendes Verb aus und verwende es im *simple present*.**

Beispiel: *Benjamin says (that) he is fourteen years old.*

say | explain | mention | add | tell the students | say | hope

a) "I come from a small town near Frankfurt."

____

b) "I have been learning English for four years."

____

c) "Before I came here on the exchange …

____

d) … I had never been to England."

____

e) "I have already learned a lot about London."

____

f) "I really love the English."

____

g) "I will come back to London one day."

____

2 Indirekte Rede – Einleitendes Verb im *past tense*

Tipp

Wenn du erst später berichtest, was jemand gesagt hat, steht das einleitende Verb der indirekten Rede in der Vergangenheit. Dann musst du auch die Zeitformen der direkten Rede verändern. Man nennt dies: Verschiebung der Zeiten – auf Englisch: *tense shift*.

Der indirekt wiedergegebene Satz wird also in die Vergangenheit „verschoben": *simple present* wird zu *simple past*, *present progressive* wird *past progressive*.

Direkte Rede	Indirekte Rede
He says: "I am fourteen years old."	*He said he was fourteen years old.*
He says: "I'm taking my dog Hunter for a walk."	*He said that he was taking his dog Hunter for a walk.*

1 ★☆ **Carl bekommt eine Nachricht von seinem deutschen Brieffreund. Gib in indirekter Rede wieder, was sein Freund erzählt. Verwende dabei die eingeklammerten Verben im *past tense*:**

Dear Carl, I have wonderful news. I'm coming to England. I can visit you! I'm looking forward to the holidays in your country. Maybe we can watch a football match of Manchester United together!
Yours, Benjamin ☺

a) Benjamin ______________________ (to write) wonderful news.

b) He ______________________ (to tell me) to England.

c) He ______________________ (to mention) me.

d) Benjamin ______________________ (to write) to the holidays.

e) He ______________________ (to hope) a football match together.

Tipp

Nicht vergessen: In der indirekten Rede musst du die Personalpronomen und die Verbformen anpassen!

2 ★☆ **Annie macht Urlaub in Deutschland und schreibt ihrer Freundin Susan eine E-Mail nach England. Susan berichtet ihrem Bruder, was Annie alles erlebt hat. Ergänze den Text und verwende dabei die indirekte Rede.**

To:
Cc:
Subject:

Dear Susan,

I hope you are fine! I'm in Tübingen today. The sun is shining. My mum and dad are doing a boat trip on the river Neckar but I'm sitting in a café and I'm relaxing ☺ I like this town a lot with its river and the beautiful old town. It's great!

Yours,
Annie

a) Annie wrote that ______________________________.

b) She said ______________ in Tübingen ______________.

c) She mentioned ______________________________.

d) She said ______________________________

but ______________ and ______________.

e) And she wrote that ______________________________.

f) She told me ______________________________.

3 ★☆ **Carl hat eine tolle Idee! Er spricht mit David und Annie über eine Reise in die USA. Hier sind ihre Meinungen und Ideen bereits in indirekter Rede wiedergegeben, allerdings mit zu vielen einleitenden Verben. Streiche die nicht passenden Verben. Manchmal ist aber auch mehr als ein Verb richtig.**

a) Carl said thought mentioned that he wanted to travel to the USA.

b) Annie and David warned thought wrote that this was a great idea, too.

c) They mentioned told agreed that they wanted to travel together.

d) David explained said answered he could ask his father who travelled to the USA some years ago.

e) Annie added hoped explained that she had lots of ideas where to go.

f) Carl agreed told said that he liked to go to New York.

g) Annie believed thought answered she loved the New England States north of New York.

h) David added told hoped that he wanted to see the Great Lakes.

4 ★☆ **Oje, Carls Gedbeutel ist weg! In der Aufregung sind die Sätze durcheinandergeraten. Verbinde die passenden Satzteile. Achte auf die richtigen einleitenden Verben.**

a) Carl told Annie	1) they had to find it soon.
b) Annie answered	2) perhaps it was in the library.
c) She added	3) that this was a good idea.
d) Carl said	4) that they could go there first.
e) Annie suggested	5) they could go on bikes to find it.
f) Carl believed	6) that he lost his purse.

5 ★★ **Carl und David unterhalten sich. Später erzählt Carl seiner Schwester Annie davon. Setze Davids Aussagen in die indirekte Rede und verwende einleitende Verben im *simple past*. Denke an das *tense shift* sowie an die sich ändernden Zeitangaben und Personalpronomen.**

a) "There is a new girl in our class, Emiliana."

David said ______________________________

b) "She comes from Equador."

____

c) "We usually walk home from school together."

____

d) "Emiliana's English isn't very good."

____

e) "That's why I'm learning Spanish at the moment."

____

f) "I like this language very much. And I like Emiliana."

____

g) "She is waiting for me in the schoolyard."

____

h) "I have to go because she is waiting for me."

____

6 ★★ **Carl, Annie und David wollen in die USA reisen. Annie und David haben sich notiert, was Freunde, die schon einmal dort waren, ihnen erzählt haben. Sie berichten nun Carl. Fülle die Lücken.**

Erik: It's a long way to travel.

Pete: Las Vegas is great.

Kyle: New Orleans is not a good place to go because it's too far south.

Connie: Mesa Verde is very interesting because you can see the Indian cave-dwellings[1].

Suzanne: Florida is beautiful, and you can go swimming there and see the alligators in Everglades National Park.

Marianne: Don't go to Kansas – it's boring.

Joey: The Great Lakes are fun.

1 cave-dwellings – Höhlenbehausungen

David: Well, Erik explained that ______________________________

______________________________,

but Pete said that ______________________________

______________________________.

Annie: That's right, but Kyle told us ______________________________

______________________________ because it

______________________________.

And Connie thought ____

____ because

____.

David: You know, I think Suzanne is not very good at geography.

She told me that ____

____ because

____

____.

Doesn't she know where Florida is?

Annie: Well, let's forget about this. Marianne told us ____________________

____ because

____.

I think that's good to know.

David: You're right. And Joey said ______________________________

____.

Maybe we can go swimming there.

Carl: So where will we go? I'll go to a travel agency and find out more tomorrow.

7 ★★ **Carl möchte gerne ein kleines Tattoo, seine Mutter ist jedoch absolut dagegen. Gib die Argumente der beiden in indirekter Rede wieder. Das einleitende Verb setzt du jeweils ins *simple past*.**

a) Carl: "I want to get a small tattoo on my back."

____

____

b) Mom: "You are much too young to get a tattoo."

____

____

c) Carl: "People who are much younger have already gotten tattoos."

____

____

d) Mom: "I don't care what other people do."

____

____

e) Carl: "There are simply no good reasons for your decision."

____

____

f) Mom: "Tattoos are bad for your health."

____

____

g) Carl: "The tattoo studio uses only safe tattoo inks *(Farben)*."

h) Mom: "If the studio isn't clean, you can still *(dennoch)* risk infections."

i) Carl: "You can come with me to the studio and see if it is clean."

j) Mom: "It can be difficult to get a job if you have a tattoo."

k) Carl: "If this is the case, I can get rid of my tattoo."

l) Mom: "That's enough! I do not allow you to get a tatoo!"

Tipp

Die Verschiebung der Zeiten folgt sowohl für die einfachen Formen *(simple forms)* wie auch für die Verlaufsformen *(progressive forms)* den gleichen Regeln.

Hier eine Übersicht über das *tense shift* in der Vergangenheit:

simple past	→	past perfect
past progressive	→	past perfect progressive
present perfect	→	past perfect **(bleibt!)**
present perfect progressive	→	past perfect progressive
past perfect progressive	→	past perfect progressive **(bleibt!)**

Bei der Umformung von direkten Rede in die indirekte Rede können folgende Formen nicht verändert werden:
- *past perfect*
- *past perfect progressive*

8 ★☆ **Ein Unfall! Ergänze die Lücken in Annies Bericht in indirekter Rede.**

a) "Matt had his basketball with him in the classroom."
b) "He wanted to play with Luke between classes."
c) "Matt threw the ball at Luke."
d) "He accidentally (versehentlich) hit the lamp."
e) "Luckily nobody was hurt."

a) Annie said that Matt ______________________________ in the classroom.

b) She added that he ______________________________ between the classes.

c) She explained that Matt ______________________________ .

d) Annie said he ______________________________ the lamp.

e) She added that luckily ______________________________ .

9 ★☆ **David hatte einen fürchterlichen Tag. Setze seinen Bericht in die indirekte Rede.**

> *I have had a really bad day! An accident happened right in front of me, so I was late for school. And I had forgotton my homework! My teacher gave us too much homework. Jayden was bullying me all the time.*

a) David said *he had had a really bad day.*

b) He explained ______________________________

______________________________.

c) He told us ______________________________.

d) David complained ______________________________.

e) He complained as well ______________________________ all the time.

10 ★☆ **Auch Annies Tag war zuerst gar nicht so toll. Aber dann... Ergänze die Sätze in der indirekten Rede.**

> *First, I missed the school bus, so I had to walk to school. But there was nobody in our classroom when I finally arrived. I was looking for my classmates when I heard them talk in the schoolyard. The headmaster had declared lessens over because of the heat!*

Annie said, that ______________ the school bus, so ______________ to walk to school. Then, there ______________ nobody in ________ classroom when she finally ______________ . She ______________ for ________ classmates when she ______________ them talk in the schoolyard. The headmaster ______________ lessons over because of the heat!

11 ★☆

Carl erzählt seinen Eltern von seinem deutschen Brieffreund Benjamin. Gib Benjamins Aussagen in der indirekten Rede wieder, setze die einleitenden Verben ins *simple past*.

explain say mention tell us add say

a) "I am fourteen years old."

Benjamin told us that he was fourteen years old.

b) "I come from a small town near Frankfurt."

____

c) "I have been learning English for four years."

____

d) "Before I came here on the exchange …

____

e) … I had never been to England."

____

f) "I have already learned a lot about London."

____

g) "I really love the English."

____

Tipp

Auch Ortsangaben und Pronomen ändern sich in der indirekten Rede.

Direkte Rede		**Indirekte Rede**
this	→	*that*
here	→	*there*

12 ★★ **David erzählt von seiner Reise nach Heidelberg. Setze seine Erzählung in die indirekte Rede. Achte dabei auf die Veränderung der Orts- und Zeitangaben.**

a) "We arrived in Heidelberg on Saturday morning. I had never been there before."

____

____

b) "In the afternoon, our whole family went to the castle."

____

c) "It was raining on Sunday so we went swimming in an indoor pool."

____

d) "My mum and I went to the zoo on Monday while my dad and my brother were doing a boat trip on the Neckar."

____

____

e) "We left Heidelberg on Tuesday."

____

f) "While our parents were booking out of the hotel (auschecken), my brother and I went for a walk in the old town."

____

____

Tipp

Achtung: Das *past perfect* kann nicht weiter zurückgesetzt werden, denn es ist die letzte Zeitstufe im Englischen. In der indirekten Rede bleiben daher das *past perfect* und das *past perfect progressive* unverändert!

David: *"I had never been there before."* → *David said he had never been there before.*

3 Zeitangaben in der indirekten Rede

Tipp

Beibehaltung der Zeitangabe

Häufig kommen in der direkten Rede Zeitangaben vor, die sich auf einen bestimmten Tag beziehen, wie *today* oder *tomorrow*. Berichtest du noch am selben Tag in indirekter Rede darüber, so ändert sich die Zeitangabe nicht.

"I will write a math test tomorrow."
She told me she would write a math test tomorrow.

Auch Zeitangaben, die sich auf einen bestimmten Monat oder ein bestimmtes Jahr beziehen, behältst du bei, wenn der betreffende Monat oder das Jahr noch nicht vorbei sind.

1 ★☆ **Tim, Davids Brieffreund, erzählt am Telefon von seiner Reise in die USA. David berichtet seinen Eltern noch am gleichen Abend davon. Schreibe in indirekter Rede, was er schon alles gemacht hat.**

Beispiel: "We have already done so much since last week."

Tim said (that) they had already done so much since last week.

a) "Yesterday we went to Venice Beach."

____

b) "Today we could choose between different activitities at school."

____

c) "So I went to American football training this afternoon."

____

d) "Sports are much more important here than they are back in Germany."

____

e) "Jacob, a boy from school, has invited me to a barbecue party tonight."

____

Tipp

Veränderung der Zeitangabe

Meist ist der Zeitpunkt, auf den sich Zeitangaben in der indirekten Rede beziehen, jedoch schon vorüber, wenn darüber berichtet wird.

"I will write a math test tomorrow."
Erzählst du erst einige Tage später, so lautet die indirekte Rede:
She told me she would write a math test the next day.

So verändern sich die Zeitangaben beim Umwandeln der direkten in die indirekte Rede:

Direkte Rede		**Indirekte Rede**
today	→	that day
tonight	→	that evening
a week/a month/a year ago	→	a week/a month/a year before a week/a month/a year earlier
last year, week, month	→	a year/week/month before; the previous year/week/month
yesterday	→	the day before
tomorrow	→	the next / following day

Annie: *"Last week we went to Berlin."*
Annie told us they had gone to Berlin a week earlier.

2 ★★ **Verwende noch einmal die Angaben aus Aufgabe 2. Schreibe nun, was David seiner Tante eine Woche später über den Anruf erzählt.**

a) ______________________________

b) ______________________________

c) ______________________________

d) ______________________________

e) ______________________________

3 ★★ **Heute, gestern, letztes Jahr – an das Ändern der Zeitangaben musst du immer denken. Setze die direkte Rede in die indirekte Rede, finde dafür unterschiedliche Verben im Einleitungssatz.**

a) David: "I played the piano yesterday."

____

b) Annie: "Today I haven't done my homework yet."

____

c) Carl: "I was ill last week so I couldn't do my homework."

____

d) Annie: "Last month I went to Berlin with all of my friends."

____

e) David: "I broke my leg last year in a car accident. That's why I can't run so far."

____

f) Annie: "Susan has invited me to a barbecue party tonight."

____

g) Carl: "Last winter I spent my holidays in Austria."

____

h) David: "Yesterday I worked in the garden."

____

Tipp

Achtung! *Could, should* und *would* verändern sich nicht beim *tense shift*!

4 ★★ **David, Carl und Annie wollen gemeinsam in die USA reisen. Annie erzählt den beiden, was ihre Familie dazu sagt. Streiche die einleitenden Verben durch, die nicht passen.**

Anna's mother **told / thought / asked** that it was a great idea to travel through America, but she also **mentioned / told / said** them to be very careful.
Anna's father was very excited and **explained / said / warned** that he had done a trip like that 30 years before.
However, he also **asked / told / explained** them to be careful, especially in the Alaskan wilderness.
Anna laughed and **explained / said / wrote** that they weren't planning on going to Alaska, so he could relax.
Her father **thought / believed / asked** that that was a good idea. He **wanted to know / wondered / thought** where they were planning on going instead.
Anna **said / answered / mentioned** that they hadn't made any plans.
Her father was very excited and he **told / said / wrote** her to visit a hundred wonderful places.
Half an hour later, Anna put down the phone and was very confused about her trip.
Then she wrote to her grandmother. She answered quickly, and in her letter she **asked / told / said** Anna that she was too young for such a trip and that she should rather stay at home.
She also **said / mentioned / explained** that America was too far away.
She **told / mentioned / asked** her to come home as fast as possible.
She also **believed / wrote / told** that America was full of gangsters and was a really dangerous place.
In the end she **warned / told / asked** Anna not to leave the house until her father could come and bring her back home.
When she showed this letter to Christopher and Erica they laughed.
They **said / asked / thought** that grandparents were the same all over the world.

4 Indirekte Rede für zukünftige Ereignisse

Tipp

Denk daran: Auch wenn über die Zukunft gesprochen wird, ändert sich die Zeit in der indirekten Rede, wenn das einleitende Verb in der Vergangenheit steht.

will	→	*would*
am/is/are going	→	*was/were going*
Direkte Rede		**Indirekte Rede**
"I will be a good teacher."	→	*She said she would be a good teacher.*
"I am going to prepare lunch."	→	*He said he was going to prepare lunch.*

1 ★☆ **Verbinde den Einleitungssatz der indirekten Rede mit dem richtigen Folgesatz.**

Beispiel: Annie says: *"I'm going to play the piano."*

Annie said
- that she were going to play the piano.
- that she were playing the piano.
- that she was going to play the piano.

a) Carl promises: *"I'll do my homework tomorrow."*

Carl promised
- he would do his homework the next day.
- he'll do his homework the next day.
- he would do his homework tomorrow.

b) Annie says: *"We're going to leave early."*

Annie said
- they are going to leave early.
- they would leave early.
- they were going to leave early.

c) David believes: *"We'll be the best football team."*

David believed
- they were the best football team.
- they would be the best football team.
- they would have been the best football team.

2 ★☆ **Geburtstag! Annie und Carl haben viel vor. Fülle die Lücken und denke dabei an das *tense shift* und passe die Zeitangaben an.**

Carl: "Mom will be 40 on Sunday."

Annie: "We'll buy some flowers for her on Saturday."

Carl: "We're going to prepare the present this evening."

Annie: "I'm going to bake a birthday cake for mom."

Carl: "We're going to have a party!"

a) Carl said ______________________________ on Sunday.

b) Annie answered that ______________________ a birthday cake for her mom.

c) Carl mentioned they ______________________ to prepare the present

______________________________.

d) Annie mentioned ______________________________ on Saturday.

e) Carl shouted that ______________________________ a party!

Tipp

Achtung! Auch bei der indirekten Rede in der Zukunft musst du die Zeitangaben der direkten Rede verändern, wenn du erst später davon berichtest:

Carl: *"I will travel to Australia next year."* → *Carl said he would travel to Australia the following year.*

Direkte Rede		**Indirekte Rede**
next year, week, month	→	the following year/week/month
tomorrow	→	the next / following day

3 ★☆

Bald sind Ferien und Carl und David machen viele Pläne. Carl erzählt seinem Vater, was sie vorhaben. Schreibe die Sätze in der indirekten Rede. Setze die einleitenden Verben ins *simple past*.

a) David and Carl: "We're going to go swimming every day!"

We said that ______________________________.

b) David: "I'll go to Will's party next month. You should come as well."

David mentioned that ______________________________ and that

I ______________________________ as well.

c) David: "I'm going to practise the guitar very often so I'll be able to play great songs."

David says ______________________________

____

d) David and Carl: "We'll stay up until 12 o'clock every evening during the next weeks!"

We said ______________________________

e) David: "We should buy a new computer game so we'll be able to play it all day long."

David suggested that we ______________________________

so we ______________________________ all day long.

Tipp

Denke daran, dass *could*, *should* und *would* sich nicht verändern, wenn die indirekte Rede gebildet wird!

4 ★★ **Annie und ihre Freundin Jessi haben auch schon Pläne für die Ferien gemacht. Annie erzählt ihrem Vater einige Zeit später, was sie vorhaben. Notiere, was die Mädchen gesagt haben und wandle die indirekte Rede wieder in direkte Rede um. Beachte die richtige Verwendung der Anführungszeichen.**

Beispiel: I said that I would visit my grandma the following week.
Annie says: "I'll visit my grandma next week."

a) Jessi told me she was going to go Will's party the following month.

Jessi tells Annie: ______________________________

____

b) Jessi added she would only go there if I went with her.

____

______________________________ *adds Jessi.*

c) We said we were going to listen to music all day long.

____

____

d) Jessi explained that she wouldn't learn anything for school in these holidays.

____

____

e) We said we were going to go to the concert of Coldplay the following month.

____

____

f) We agreed that we would have wonderful summer holidays that year.

____

____

5 Indirekte Fragen

Tipp

Die Satzstellung von Fragen in der indirekten Rede ist die gleiche wie in Aussagesätzen:

Subjekt – Prädikat – Objekt (SPO)

Entscheidungsfragen werden mit *if* oder *whether* eingeleitet, bei Fragen mit Fragewort wird das Fragenwort beibehalten. Das *tense shift* gilt natürlich hier genauso.

"Have you ever travelled alone?" → He asked if/whether I had ever travelled alone.

"When does the next bus to Manchester leave?" → She asked when the next bus to Manchester left.

1 ★☆ **Benjamin, Carls Brieffreund, hat viele Fragen an Carl. Carl erzählt Annie später, was Benjamin alles wissen wollte. Fülle die Lücken bei den indirekten Fragen und achte auf die richtige Satzstellung.**

Beispiel: *"How are you today?" – Benjamin wanted to know how I was.*

a) "Do you still have to do your homework?"

Benjamin asked if ______________________________ to do my homework

b) "Are you studying for your maths lesson right now?"

He asked whether ________________ for my maths lesson at that moment.

c) "When are you going to visit me in Germany?"

He asked me when ______________________________ in Germany.

d) "Where does your father work?"

Benjamin asked where ______________________________.

e) "Do you play an instrument?"

He asked if ______________________________.

2 ★☆ **Annie verbringt das Wochenende bei ihrer Freundin Susan. Annies Vater hat noch einige Fragen. Annie erzählt Susan, was ihr Vater gefragt hat. Bringe die Fragen in die indirekte Rede.**

Beispiel: "Are you staying at Susans house?"

Dad wanted to know if we were staying at your house.

a) "Will Susans parents be at home?"

Dad asked ______________________

b) "What are you going to do on Saturday evening?"

Dad wondered ______________________

c) "Are you going to go to the cinema?"

Dad wanted to know ______________________

d) "Do you need some money?"

Dad asked ______________________

Tipp

Du kannst indirekte Fragen mit folgenden Verben einleiten: *ask, want to know, wonder.*

3 ★☆ **Carl und David gehen zu einer Party. Davids Mutter Mrs Hunter möchte noch einiges wissen. Setze ihre Fragen in die indirekte Rede.**

Mrs Hunter: "How many of your friends will come? Will you play music? Won't it be too loud? When will the party end?"

a) *Mrs Hunter asked* ______________________

b) *She wanted to know* ______________________

c) *Mrs Hunter wondered* ______________________

d) *She asked* ______________________

4 ★☆ **Annie war im Reisebüro, um sich über ihre geplante Amerikareise zu erkundigen. Am nächsten Tag erzählt sie Carl und David, was sie erfahren hat. Bringe die direkte in die indirekte Rede und fülle die Lücken im Text.**

1. Are you old enough to travel alone?

2. Do your parents know about your plans?

3. When do you want to leave?

4. How much time do you have for your trip?

5. How much money do you want to spend?

6. Will you go by train or by bus?

7. Do you want to visit National Parks or cities?

Carl: What did you find out, Annie?

Annie: Not much really. The lady just asked a lot of questions and when I couldn't answer some of them, she told me to go home, find out, and then come back.

David: Alright. What did she ask?

Annie: First, she asked if we were old enough to travel alone.

When I said "yes", she ______________________________

______________________________.

I replied that it had even been our parents' idea. That surprised her, but she

went on and ______________________________

______________________________.

I told her that we had all summer. I think she was quite impressed but then she

asked all the questions we hadn't talked about yet. She ______________

____

then she ______________________________

______________________________.

When I told her that we didn't know, she sighed but went on and ______________

____

and ______________________________

______________________________.

Again I had to tell her that we didn't know. She told me to go home and talk to you about these questions.

5 ★☆ **Die Klasse von Carl hat viele Fragen an den deutschen Austauschschüler Benjamin. Gib sie in indirekter Rede wieder.**

a) "Do you like our school?"

The students asked if/weather Benjamin liked their school.

b) "Do you have a girlfriend?"

They wanted to know ______

c) "Have you ever had a date *(Verabredung)* with an English girl?"

The boys and girls asked ______

d) "Are there any differences between Germans and the English?"

Jacob's classmates wanted to find out ______

e) "Have you ever been to a school dance?"

They asked ______

f) "Have you seen a lot of England yet?"

One of their questions was ______

g) "Do you know any English people in Germany?"

The students were interested in finding out ______

6 ★☆

Direkt nachdem Benjamin in London angekommen ist, hat sein amerikanischer Cousin einige Fragen an ihn. Schreibe diese in indirekter Rede. Das einleitende Verb setzt du dazu immer ins *simple past*.

Beispiel: Did you have any problems during the flight?"

Benjamin's cousin asked if he had had any problems during the flight.

a) "Did you sleep during the flight?"

b) "Did you get a seat next to your friend on the plane?"

c) "Was the food on board the plane all right?"

d) "Did the stewardess speak German?"

e) "Did your host family meet you at the airport in London?"

f) "Do you feel comfortable *(wohl)* with your host family?"

g) "Are you sharing a room with your host brother?"

Tipp

Denke daran, dass du Entscheidungsfragen, also Fragen ohne Fragewort, in der indirekten Rede mit *if* und *wether* einleitest.

Tipp

Bei Ergänzungsfragen in der indirekten Rede, also bei Fragen mit Fragewort, behältst du das Fragewort bei.

7 ★★ **Hier findest du einige Fragen, die du bei einer Verabredung besser nicht stellen solltest. Setze sie in die indirekte Rede. Beginne deine Sätze jeweils mit *Never ask* ... Denke daran, dass du in diesem Fall die Zeit nicht verschiebst.**

Beispiel: "Why are you wearing such an awful T-shirt?"

Never ask why your date (Datingpartner) is wearing such an awful T-shirt.

a) "Where did you get your terrible haircut?"

____

b) "Why can't you tell me anything more interesting?"

____

c) "When can I go home?"

____

d) "Why did you choose such a boring movie?"

____

e) "When will you stop getting on my nerves?"

____

f) "What can I do to finish this date as quickly as possible?"

____

g) "Why didn't I say no when you asked me out?"

____

8 ★★ **Benjamin stellt bei seiner Verabredung mit Nicky, einem Mädchen aus Carls Klasse, die richtigen Fragen. Gib diese in indirekter Rede wieder. Das einleitende Verb setzt du immer ins *simple past*.**

Beispiel: "What would you like to drink?"

Benjamin asked Nicky what she would like to drink.

a) "Where did you buy this fantastic dress?"

____

b) "What do you want to know about me?"

____

c) "What do you usually do on weekends?"

____

d) "How did you learn to speak German so well?"

____

e) "Who do you hang out with at school?"

____

f) "What kind of movies do you like?"

____

g) „What kind of sports do you like?"

____

h) "When will I see you again?"

____

9 ★★ **Hier geht es um typische Fragen eines Polizisten direkt nach einem Verkehrsunfall. Diesmal musst du die indirekte Rede in direkte Rede "zurückübersetzen". Kreuze die Version an, die dem indirekten Satz am besten entspricht.**

a) The police officer wanted to know who had been driving the car at the time of the accident.

- ☐ "Who was driving the car at the time of the accident?"
- ☐ "Who has been driving the car at the time of the accident?"

b) He asked if anybody had been injured (verletzt).

- ☐ "Is anybody injured?"
- ☐ "Has anybody been injured?"

c) He tried to find out why the man hadn't stopped at the traffic light (Ampel).

- ☐ "Why didn't you stop at the traffic light?"
- ☐ "Why did you stop at the traffic light?"

d) He wanted to know if we had seen any other vehicle involved in the accident.

- ☐ "Have you seen any other vehicle involved in the accident?"
- ☐ "Did you see any other vehicle involved in the accident?"

6 Indirekte Aufforderungen

1 ★☆ **David beschwert sich. Schreibe in indirekter Rede, was sein Vater ihm verboten oder aufgetragen hat.**

a) "Do your homework properly."

My Dad told me to do my homework properly. ____

b) "Don't eat so much sweets again!"

He told me ____ so much sweets again.

c) "Don't go to the disco."

He told me ____ to the disco.

d) "Stay in your room!"

Dad told me ____ in my room.

e) "Don't drink alcohol."

He told me ____ drink alcohol.

Tipp

Um Befehle, Bitten und Aufforderungen in indirekter Rede wiederzugeben, verwendest du eine Infinitivkonstruktion mit *to*.
Diese besteht aus Verb + Objekt + Infinitiv mit *to*.
Die verneinte Form des Infinitivs lautet *not to:*

The teacher told the students to be quiet.
He told them not to run around.

Das Objekt ist immer die Person, an die sich die Aufforderung richtet.

2 ★☆ **Carl bekommt allerhand Aufträge von seiner Mutter. Wähle passende einleitende Verben, setze sie ins *simple past* und bilde indirekte Aufforderungssätze.**

tell | warn | advise | ask | remind

a) "Help me wash the car!"

Mum asked me ____________________

b) "Tidy up your room!"

She ____________________

c) "Prepare dinner!"

____

d) "Don't watch too much television."

____

e) "Practise the guitar for half an hour."

____

f) "Help me in the garden."

____

Tipp

Indirekte Aufforderungssätze werden häufig durch Verben wie *tell, ask, warn, advise* und *remind* eingeleitet.

Denke daran, auch bei indirekten Aufforderungssätzen die Personalpronomen und die Zeitangaben anzupassen!

3 ★★ **Annie und ihre Klasse fährt zum Schüleraustausch nach Deutschland. Ihr Lehrer erteilt noch einmal einige Anweisungen. Forme diese in indirekte Aufforderungssätze um, wähle verschiedene einleitende Verben und setze sie ins *simple past*.**

Beispiel: "Let me know about any problems."

Mr Brown advised the students to let him know about any problems.

a) "Remember that many things are different in Germany."

b) "Always be polite to your host families."

c) "Don't behave selfishly."

d) "Don't break your host parents' rules."

e) "Take warm clothes with you."

f) "Take part in (teilnehmen an) your host families' activities."

g) "Bring your host families some small presents."

____

____

h) "Try to speak some simple German sentences."

____

____

i) "Don't forget your dictionaries."

____

____

4 ★★ **Carls Lehrerin besteht darauf, dass bestimmte Regeln eingehalten werden. Forme diese Regeln in indirekte Aufforderungssätze um.**

a) "Show respect (Respekt) to your fellow classmates."

The teacher asked the students ______________________________

____

b) "Don't distract each other."

She advised them ______________________________

____

c) "Don't talk if it's not your turn."

She told them ______________________________

____

d) "Never laugh about a wrong answer."

She reminded them ______________________________

____

e) "Don't tell me lies about your missing homework."

She warned them ______________________________

____

f) "Don't hit each other."

She told them ______________________________

____

g) "Keep the classroom clean and tidy."

She asked them ______________________________

____

h) "Don't make fun of your fellow classmates."

She advised them ______________________________

____

i) "Come to the lessons on time."

She reminded them ______________________________

____

j) "Turn off your cell phones (Handys) during lessons."

She warned them ______________________________

____

5 ★★ **Die große Reise in die USA rückt näher. Annie und Carl haben David aufgetragen, einige Informationen im Internet zu recherchieren. Setze ihre Wünsche in die indirekte Rede und benutze diese einleitenden Verben:**

ask someone to do sth tell so to do sth want sb to do sth.

Carl:

1. Please find out what a Greyhound ticket from here to New York costs.
2. Make sure to check if we can get off as often as we want to.
3. Please see if you can find out more about Mesa Verde.
4. See what there is on Chicago.
5. Oh, and hurry up, I want to check my e-mail.

Annie:

1. Please check where we can go by train.
2. Oh yes, and find out more about Kansas.
3. Check on chat-rooms to find out more about travelling in the US.
4. Oh, and write an e-mail to the lady at the travel agency and tell her that she was very unfriendly, and that we won't come back.

David: OK, let's start:

1. Carl asked me ______________________________

______________________________.

2. He also ______________________________

______________________________.

3. Then ______________________________

______________________________.

4. He also ______________________________

______________________________.

5. Finally, ____

____. Idiot!

Annie also had some interesting ideas. Let's see:

1. First she wanted me ____

____.

2. Then she ____

____.

Why is she interested in Kansas? It's so boring there. Anyway:

3. She also ____

____.

That was a good idea.

4. Finally, she ____

____.

Alright, that's it then.

Tipp

Gefühlsausdrücke oder Höflichkeitsfloskeln wie

please, oh

etc. kann man beim Umwandeln in die indirekte Rede in der Regel weglassen.

7 Modalverben in der indirekten Rede

Tipp

Achtung! Auch die Modalverben ändern sich, wenn die direkte in die indirekte Rede umgewandelt wird, denn für sie gilt das *tense shift* ebenso.

can	→	*could, be able to, be allowed to*	*needn't*	→	*not have to*
must	→	*have to*	*mustn't*	→	*not be allowed to*
may	→	*be allowed to*	*shall*	→	*should*

Denk daran, dass *could, would* und *should* nicht verändert werden!

"You can call me!" *He said I could call him.*
"I could travel to Berlin next weekend." *He said he could travel to Berlin next weekend.*

1 ★☆ **David fährt in die Ferien und bittet Annie, sich um seinen Hund Hunter zu kümmern. Annie freut sich und erzählt gleich Carl davon. Bilde die indirekte Rede und achte auf die Modalverben.**

a) "You must feed Hunter his favourite food or he won't eat it."

David said I had to feed Hunter his favourite food or he wouldn't eat it.

b) "You should go for a walk with him twice a day."

He said ____________________ for a walk with him twice a day.

c) "You can brush Hunter if you want to. He loves it."

He added ____________________ Hunter if I ____________________

because he ____________________ it.

d) "Hunter could get angry if you don't pay attention to him from time to time."

He warned me that ____________________ if I ____________________

attention to him from time to time.

e) "You needn't let him sleep on the sofa."

David told me that ____________________ sleep on the sofa.

2 ★★ **Annie hätte auch gerne einen Hund. Sie spricht mit ihrer Freundin Susan darüber und erzählt später ihrer Mutter, was Susan alles gesagt hat. Schreibe die Sätze in der indirekten Rede.**

a) "You can jog with your dog every day, so you would be really fit!"

Susan said ______________________________

b) "But you must go for a walk with him twice a day…"

____

c) "You could teach your dog some tricks. That would be funny!"

____

d) "You mustn't let him sleep in your bed."

____

3 ★★ **Susan hat eine zahme Ratte namens Carlos. Sie erklärt ihrer Mutter, was sie alles tun soll, während sie zum Schüleraustausch in Deutschland ist. Schreibe in indirekter Rede, was Susans Mutter beachten muss.**

a) "You should take Carlos out of his cage every day."

Susan said I ______________________________

b) "Carlos must not eat sweets, you know!"

____

c) "You must clean his cage once a week."

____

d) "Carlos could bite you if you aren't careful."

____

e) "You may show him to my cousins if they want to see him."

____

8 Gemischte Aufgaben

1 ★☆ **In einer Jugendherberge kann man viele verschiedene Menschen treffen. Hier kannst du lesen, was sie alles zu erzählen haben. Ordne die direkte Rede der indirekten Rede auf der nächsten Seite zu.**

1. I may come back very late tonight.
2. Can I have the keys to my room, please!
3. Have you ever travelled alone?
4. I like long bus rides.
5. My parents will take me to Hawaii next summer.
6. I spent last winter in Europe with my friends.
7. When does the next bus to New York leave?
8. I'm going to stay in the cheapest hotel in Manhattan.
9. Don't tell my girlfriend that I went out late.

a) *David:* A little boy told someone that he liked long bus rides. 4

b) *Annie:* An older traveller mentioned that he had spent the previous* winter in Europe with his friends. ☐

c) *David:* A girl in a dress said that she might come back very late that night. ☐

d) *Annie:* A backpacker asked his friend when the next bus to New York left. ☐

e) *David:* A young girl said her parents would take her to Hawaii the following summer. ☐

f) *Annie:* A drunk guy asked the receptionist to give him the keys to his room. ☐

g) *David:* A good-looking teenager told his friend not to tell his girlfriend that he had gone out late. ☐

h) *Annie:* A girl with red hair asked someone whether she had ever travelled alone. ☐

i) *David:* Another very dirty-looking guy said that he was going to stay in the cheapest hotel in Manhattan. ☐

***previous** – vorherig(e)

2 ★☆ **Hier ist aber ein Durcheinander. Verbinde die Angaben, wie du sie von der direkten zur indirekten Rede ändern musst.**

Direkte Rede	Indirekte Rede
next year	that day
we	he/she
here	they
last week	there
today	I (Subjekt)/me (Objekt) / we (Subjekt)/me (Objekt)
next year	the day before
I	then, at that time
this week	his/hers
you	the previous week
my	the following day
tomorrow	that week
yesterday	the following year

3 ★☆ **Annie stellt Susan Fragen zu ihrer Klassenreise nach Edinburgh. Schreibe sie in der indirekten Rede auf.**

a) "Where did you stay in Edinburgh?"

Annie asked where we ______________________________

b) "Have you visited many museums?"

____

c) "Where had you been before you went to Edinburgh?"

____

4 ★☆

Carl und David haben in nächster Zeit viel vor. Schreibe in direkter Rede auf, was in indirekter Rede hier geschrieben steht.

Beispiel: Carl said he was going to the disco that evening. –
Carl: "I'm going to the disco this evening."

a) David asked if Carl was going to go to the concert of Imagine Dragons with him.

____

____

b) Carl said he would love to go to that concert if David went there as well.

____

____

c) David asked if Carl's mom would drive them to the concert.

____

d) Carl wanted to know if they were going to practice the guitar together in the holidays.

____

____

e) David answered that they would improve their guitar skills a lot if they did.

____

____

f) Carl promised they would become famous rock stars if they continued practicing that much.

____

____

5 ★☆

**Davids Vater möchte wissen, was David den Tag über gemacht hat.
Am nächsten Tag in der Schule erzählt David Carl davon. Setze seine Fragen in die indirekte Rede.**

a) "What were you doing today while I had to work?"

My dad wanted to know ______________________________

____

b) "Did you go to your guitar lesson?"

____

c) "Have you been in the skater park?"

____

d) "Have you been hanging around with Carl the whole day?"

____

____

e) "When did you do your homework? Did you have any problems?"

____

____

f) "Why haven't you prepared dinner yet?"

____

____

6 ★★ **Bringe diese Meinungen über das Reisen in die indirekte Rede.**

a) "Travelling by train is dangerous because trains are too fast."

A man in 1875 ____

____.

b) "I'm afraid of travelling by plane. My cousin died in a plane crash five years ago."

Last year a friend of mine ____

____

____.

c) "My mother went to America by ship last year and she loved it."

One of my classmates ____

____.

d) "I'm going to fly to the moon as soon as possible because I hate life here."

My pen friend from Australia ____

____

____.

e) "Do you know how bad it is for the environment that everybody is flying around the world all the time?"

My brother ____

____

____.

7 ★★ **Auf der Suche nach Ideen für ihre Amerikareise sucht Annie in einem Internetforum nach Erfahrungsberichten. Sie erzählt Carl und David einige Tage später davon. Fülle die Lücken.**

Jason (2004)	*You* should definitely travel through Kansas, *I* have lived *here* all *my* life and *I* think it's great!
Anne (2005)	Don't go to Chicago: *I* hate it *here*. *I* moved *here a year ago*. All *you* will see *here* are cars, cars, cars and cars.
Allison (2007)	Mesa Verde is the greatest place of all. *We* arrived *here yesterday* and I hope *we* will stay until *Tuesday*. That's when there will be a special guided tour of the Native American sites.
Joey (2005)	*My* sister came back from her trip *three days ago*, and she was very excited about the Great Lakes. *I* think she is crazy because *I* was there *last winter* and it was freezing cold.

Annie: Alright, here's what I found out: A guy called Jason wrote that ________________ should definitely travel through Kansas. He said that ________________ had lived ________________ all ________________ life and ________________ thought it was great! Unfortunately he didn't tell us what was great. Well, then there was a girl called Anne. She warned us not to go to Chicago. She said that ________________ hated it ________________ and that ________________ had moved ________________________________

________________ . She explained that all ________________

would see ________________ would be cars.

Then there was Allison. She was in Mesa Verde, and wrote that it was the

greatest place of all. ________________ had arrived ________________

________________ and ________________ hoped that ________________

would stay until ________________________________ . That was when there

would be a special guided tour of the Native American sites. That sounds good.

And finally there was a note by a guy called Joey. He said that ________________

sister had come back from her trip ________________________________ and

that she had been very excited about the Great Lakes. ________________ thinks

she was crazy because ________________ had been there ________________

________________ and it had been freezing cold.

So what do you think?

8 ★★ **Fünf Jahre nach Annies, Carls und Davids Reise durch die USA erzählen sie sich mal wieder, was sie alles erlebt haben. Schreibe die folgenden Sätzen in indirekter Rede.**

1. I have lost everything, in the casino. Can you please give me some money?

2. My parents forgot me here, in the desert. Can I come with you?

3. I will stay and live here in this cave. In three years you will all understand why.

4. Sure, I can give you a ride in my fantastic car, ladies – but I don't take guys.

5. Have you thought about God and about your lives? Someone might ask you soon.

6. If you kiss here, you will find everlasting love.

1. *David*: Do you remember the guy in Vegas?

   Annie: Yes, – he told us ______________________________

   and ______________________________.

2. *Carl*: Oh, yes. That was the girl in Death Valley. She ______________________________

   ____

   and ______________________________.

3. *David*: Great. I loved the hippie woman. What did she say?

   Annie: She ______________________________

   ____

   and ______________________________.

4. *Carl*: Wow! That was the "super cool" idiot with his fancy car.

   David: Yes, he ______________________________

   ____

   but he also ______________________________.

5. *Carl*: Yes, that was interesting. That was the priest in Colorado.

   He ______________________________

   ____

   and ______________________________.

   That was a little scary.

9 ★★ **Carl und sein Vater haben sich wegen einiger Fotos gestritten. Carl erzählt seinen Freunden einige Tage später davon. Korrigiere die Fehler, die er dabei macht. Manche Wörter fehlen, manche sind falsch.**

Father: Where are the pictures of my trip through America?
Carl: I haven't seen them.
Father: Don't be stupid. I'm sure you had them yesterday.
Carl: I'm really not interested in your pictures.
Father: I always keep them in my cupboard, but they aren't here now.
Mother: Look, Henry – why don't you take the ones right in front of you and leave your son alone?
Father: Hmm, that might be a good idea. Thank you, darling.

1. Yesterday my father told me where the pictures of his trip through America were.

   ____

2. I answered that I will not see them.

   ____

3. Then he told me not to be stupid and added that he was sure he had had them the day after.

   ____

4. I told that I really wasn't interested in his pictures.

   ____

5. Then dad said that he always kept them in her cupboard, but they weren't there.

   ____

6. Luckily, my mother came and wondered him why he didn't take the ones right in front of him and left me alone.

   ____

7. My dad warned that that might be a good idea and thanked my mother.

   ____

1 Direct und Indirect Speech – Einleitendes Verb im *present tense*

1 "I' tired," says Carl.
Mrs Brown asks: "Didn't you sleep well?"
Carl explains: "I've read such an exciting book yesterday, so I went to bed late last night."
Mrs Brown tells him: "Well, you shouldn't read that much this evening. Otherwise you'll be tired tomorrow, too."

2 b) She tells me it's/Edinburgh is an amazing town.
c) She thinks there are lots of wonderful ancient buildings.
d) She mentions that she has to visit the castle this afternoon.
e) She says she likes the town.

3 Die einleitenden Verben können auch in anderer Reihenfolge verwendet werden.
a) He adds (that) he comes from a small town near Frankfurt.
b) He explains (that) he has been learning English for four years.
c) He tells the students (that) before he came here on the exchange …
d) … he had never been to England.
e) He mentions (that) he has already learned a lot about London.
f) He explains (that) he really loves the Englisch.
g) He hopes (that) he will come back to London one day.

2 Indirekte Rede – Einleitendes Verb im *past tense*

1 a) Benjamin wrote that he had wonderful news.
b) He told me he was coming to England.
c) He mentioned he could visit me.
d) Benjamin wrote that he was looking forward to the holidays.
e) He hoped that we could watch a football match together.

2 a) Annie wrote that she hoped I was fine.
b) She said she was in Tübingen that day.
c) She mentioned that the sun was shining.
d) She said her mum and dad were doing a boat trip on the river Neckar but she was sitting in a café and she was relaxing.
e) She wrote she liked that town a lot with its river and the beautiful old town.
f) She told me that was great.

3 a) Carl said/mentioned that he wanted to travel to the USA.
b) Annie and David thought that this was a great idea, too.
c) They agreed that they wanted to travel together.
d) David explained/said he could ask his father who travelled to the USA some years ago.
e) Annie added/explained that she had lotsof ideas where to go.
f) Carl told /said that he liked to go to New York.
g) Annie answered she loved the New England States north of New York.
h) David added that he wanted to see the Great Lakes.

4 a – 6; b – 1; c – 5; d – 2; e – 4; f – 3

5 a) David said that there wais a new girl in his class, Emiliana.
b) He told me she came from Equador.
c) He mentioned they usually walked home from school together.
d) He said that Emiliana's English wasn't very good.
e) He explained that was why he was learning Spanish at the moment.
f) David told me he liked this language very much and he liked Emiliana.
g) He hoped that she was waiting for him in the schoolyard.
h) He explained he had to go because she was waiting for him.

6 *David:* Well, Erik explained that it was a long way to travel, but Pete said that Las Vegas was great.
Annie: That's right, but Kyle told us that New Orleans wasn't a good place to go because it was too far south. Yes, hmmm, and Connie, oh yes, she thought Mesa Verde was interesting because we could see the Indian cave-dwellings.
David: You know, I think Suzanne is not very good at geography. She told me that Florida was beautiful because we could go swimming there. Doesn't she know where Florida is?
Annie: Well, let's forget about this. Marianne told us not to go to Kansas because it was boring. I think that's good to know.
David: You're right. And Joey said that the Great Lakes were fun. Maybe we can go swimming there.
Carl: So where will we go? I'll go to a travel agency and find out more tomorrow.

7 Hier sind jeweils auch andere einleitende Verben möglich.
a) Carl said (that) he wanted to get a small tattoo on his back.
b) His mom answered (that) he was much too young to get a tattoo.
c) Carl said (that) people who were much younger had already gotten a tattoo.
d) His mom answered (that) she did not / didn't care what other people did.
e) Carl told his mom (that) there were simply no good reasons for her decision.
f) His mom explained (that) tattoos were bad for his health.
g) Carl told his mom (that) the tattoo studio used only safe tattoo inks.
h) His mom said (that) if the studio was not / wasn't clean, he could still risk infections.
i) Carl offered his mom (that) she could come with him to the studio and see if it was clean.
j) His mom answered (that) it could be difficult to get a job if he had a tattoo.
k) Carl told her (that) if that was the case, he could get rid of his tattoo.
l) His mom said that this was enough and that she did not allow him to get a tatoo.

8 a) Annie said that Matt had had his basketball with him in the classroom.
b) She added that he had wanted to play with Luke between classes.
c) She explained that Matt had thrown the ball at Luke.
d) Annie said he had accidentally hit the lamp.
e) She added that luckily nobody had been hurt.

9 a) David said he had had a really bad day.
b) He explained that an accident had happened right in front of him, so he had been late for school.
c) He told us that he had forgotten his homework.
d) David complained that his teacher had given them too much homework.
e) He complained as well that Jayden had been bullying him all the time.

10 Annie said that she had missed the school bus, first, so she had had to walk to school. She said there had been nobody in their classroom when she finally had arrived. She said that she had been looking for her classmates when she heard them talk in the schoolyard. She explained that the headmaster had declared lessons over because of the heat.

11 Die einleitenden Verben können auch in anderer Reihenfolge verwendet werden.
a) He said that he was fourteen years old.
b) He added (that) he came from a small town near Frankfurt.
c) He explained (that) he had been learning English for four years.
d) He told us (that) before he had come here with the exchange …
e) … he had never been to England before.
f) He mentioned (that) he had already learned a lot about London.
g) He explained (that) he really loved the Englisch.

12 a) David said they had arrived in Heidelberg on Saturday morning. He told me he had never been there before.
b) He added that his whole family had gone to the castle in the afternoon.
c) He explained that it had been raining on Sunday so they had gone swimming in a huge indoor swimming pool.
d) He said his mum and he had gone to the zoo on Monday while his dad and his brother had been doing a boat trip on the Neckar.
e) He added that they had left Heidelberg on Tuesday.
f) He said while their parents had been booking out of the hotel, his brother and he had gone for a walk in the old town.

3 Zeitangaben in der indirekten Rede

1 Hier sind jeweils auch andere einleitende Verben möglich.
a) He told me (that) he had gone to Venice Beach yesterday.
b) He explained (that) they could choose between different activities at school today.
c) He said (that) he had gone to American football training this afternoon.
d) He thought (that) sports were much more important here than they were back in Germany.
e) He said (that) Jacob, a boy from school, had invited him to a barbecue party tonight.

2 Hier ändern sich gegenüber Aufgabe 6 nur die Zeitangaben.
a) yesterday → the day before
b) (keine Änderung)
c) today → that day
d) this afternoon → that afternoon
e) (keine Änderung)
f) tonight → that night
g) tomorrow → until the following day
h) tomorrow → the following day

3
a) David said he had played the piano the day before.
b) Annie told me that day she hadn't done her homework yet.
c) Carl mentioned he had been ill the previous week so he couldn't do his homework.
d) Annie said that the month before she had gone to Berlin with all of her friends.
e) David explained he had broken his leg the year before in a car accident and that was why he couldn't run so far.
f) Annie told me that Susan had invited her to a barbecue party that night.
g) Carl mentioned that the previous winter he had spent his holidays in Austria.
h) David said that the day before he had worked in the garden.

4 Anna's mother thought that it was a great idea to travel through America, but she also told them to be very careful.
Anna's father was very excited and explained / said that he had done a trip like that 30 years before. However, he also asked / told them to be careful, especially in the Alaskan wilderness.
Anna laughed and explained / said that they weren't planning on going to Alaska, so he could relax.
Her father thought / believed that that was a good idea. He wanted to know /
wondered where they were planning on going instead.
Anna said / answered that they hadn't made any plans.
Her father was very excited and he told her to visit a hundred wonderful places.
Half an hour later, Anna put down the phone and was very confused about her trip.
Then she wrote to her grandmother. She answered quickly, and in her letter she told Anna that she was too young for such a trip and that she should rather stay at home.
She also said that America was too far away.
She told / asked her to come home as fast as possible.
She also believed / wrote that America was full of gangsters and was a really dangerous place.
In the end she warned / told / asked Anna not to leave the house until her father could come and bring her back home.
When she showed this letter to Christopher and Erica they laughed. They said / thought that grandparents were the same all over the world.

4 Indirekte Rede für zukünftige Ereignisse

1
a) Carl promised he would do his homework the next day.
b) Annie said they were going to leave early.
c) David believed they would be the best football team.

2
a) Carl said (that) Mom would be 40 on Sunday.
b) Annie answered that she was going to bake a birthday cake for her mom.
c) Carl mentioned they were going to prepare the present that evening.
d) Annie mentioned they would buy some flowers for her on Saturday.
e) Carl shouted that they were going to have a party!

3
a) We said that we were going to go swimming every day!
b) David mentioned that he would go to Will's party next month and that I should come as well.
c) David says that he was going to practise the guitar very often so he would be able to play great songs.
d) We said that we would stay up until 12 o'clock every evening during the following weeks.
e) David suggested that we should buy a new computer game so we would be able to play it all day long.

4
a) Jessi tells Annie: "I am going to go Will's party the next month."
b) Jessi adds: "I would only go there if you went with me."
c) Annie and Jessi say: "We are going to listen to music all day long."
d) Jessi explains: "I won't learn anything for school in these holidays."
e) Annie and Jessi say: "We are going to go to the concert of Coldplay the next month."
f) Jessi and Annie agree: "We will have wonderful summer holidays this year!"

5 Indirekte Fragen

1
a) He asked whether I still had to do my homework.
b) He asked if I was studying for my maths lesson at that moment.
c) He asked when I was going to visit him in Germany.
d) Benjamin asked where my father/dad worked.
e) He asked if I played an instrument.

2
a) Dad asked if your parents would be at home.
b) Dad wondered what we were going to do on Saturday evening.
c) Dad wanted to know whether we were going to goto the cinema.
d) Dad asked if I needed some money.

3
a) Mrs Hunter asked how many of our friends would come.
b) She wanted to know if we would play music..
c) Mrs Hunter wondered whether it wouldn't be too loud.
d) She asked whether when the party would end.

4 Die einleitenden Frageverben sind frei austauschbar.
Annie: First she asked if we were old enough to travel alone (1).
When I said "yes", she wondered whether our parents knew about our plans (2).
I replied that it had even been our parents' idea. That surprised her, but she went on and wanted to know how much time we had for our trip (3). I told her that we had all summer. I think she was quite impressed but then she asked all the questions we haven't talked about yet. She asked when we wanted to leave (4), then she wondered how much money we wanted to spend (5).
When I told her that we didn't know, she sighed but went on and asked whether we would go by train or by bus (6) and whether we wanted to visit National Parks or cities (7). Again I had to tell her that we didn't know. She told me to go home and talk to you about these questions.

5
b) They wanted to know if / whether he had a girlfriend.
c) The boys and girls asked if / whether he had ever had a date with an English girl.
d) Jacob's classmates wanted to find out if / whether there were any differences between Germans and English.
e) They asked if / whether he had ever been to a school dance.
f) One of their questions was if / whether he had seen a lot of England yet.
g) The students were interested in finding out if / whether he knew any English people in Europe.

6 Hier sind jeweils auch andere einleitende Verben möglich.
a) He wanted to know if / whether he had slept during the flight.
b) He asked if / whether he had got / had gotten a seat next to his friend on the plane.
c) He wanted to know if / whether the food on board the plane had been all right.
d) He asked if / whether the stewardess had spoken German.
e) He asked if / whether his host family had met him at the airport in LA.
f) He wanted to know if / whether he felt comfortable with his host family.
g) He asked if he was sharing a room with his host brother.

7
a) Never ask where your date got his / her terrible haircut.
b) Never ask why he / she can't tell you anything more interesting.
c) Never ask when you can go home.
d) Never ask why he / she chose such a boring movie.
e) Never ask when he / she will stop getting on your nerves.
f) Never ask what you can do to finish that date as quickly as possible.
g) Never ask why you didn't say no when he / she asked you out.

8 Hier sind jeweils auch andere einleitende Verben möglich.
a) Benjamin asked Nicky where she had bought that fantastic dress.
b) He asked her what she wanted to know about him.
c) He wanted to know what she usually did on week-ends.
d) He wondered how she had learned to speak German so well.
e) He asked who(m) she hung out with at school.
f) He wanted to know what kind of movies she liked.
g) He asked her when he would see her again.

9
a) "Who was driving the car at the time of the accident?"
b) "Has anybody been injured?"
c) "Why didn't you stop at the traffic light?"
d) "Have you seen any other vehicle involved in the accident?"

6 Indirekte Aufforderungen

1 Hier sind jeweils auch andere einleitende Verben möglich.
a) My dad told me to do my homework properly.
b) He told me not to eat so much sweets.
c) He told me not to go to the disco.
d) Dad told me to stay in my room.
e) He told me not to drink alcohol.

2
a) Mum asked me to help her wash the car.
b) She reminded me to tidy up my room.
c) She told me to prepare dinner.
d) She warned me not to watch too much television.
e) Mum advised me to practice the guitar for half an hour.
f) She asked me to help her in the garden.

3 Hier darfst du natürlich in jedem Satz auch andere passende einleitende Verben benutzen!
a) He told them to remember that many things were different in Germany.
b) He warned them to always be polite to their host families.
c) He reminded them not to behave selfishly.
d) He advised them not to break their host parents' rules.
e) He reminded them to take warm clothes with them.
f) He asked them to take part in their host families' activities.

g) He told them to bring their host families some small presents.
h) He advised them to try to speak some simple German sentences.
i) He reminded them not to forget their dictionaries.

4 a) The teacher asked the students to show respect to their fellow classmates.
b) She advised them not to distract each other.
c) She told them not to talk if it was not / wasn't their turn.
d) She reminded them never to laugh about a wrong answer.
e) She warned them not to tell her lies about their missing homework.
f) She told them not to hit each other.
g) She asked them to keep the classroom clean and tidy.
h) She advised them not to make fun of their fellow classmates.
i) She reminded them to come to the lessons on time.
j) She warned them to turn off their cell phones during lessons.

5 Die einleitenden Verben sind auch hier frei austauschbar.
1. Carl asked me to find out what a Greyhound ticket from here to New York costs / will cost.
2. He also wanted me to check if we could / can / will be able to get off as often as we want to.
3. Then he asked me to find out more about Mesa Verde.
4. He also told me to see what there was on Chicago.
5. Finally he wanted me to hurry up because he wanted to check his e-mail. Idiot!

Annie also had some interesting ideas. Let's see:
1. First she wanted me to check where we could go by train.
2. Then she asked me to find out more about Kansas. Why is she interested in Kansas? It's so boring there. Anyway:
3. She also told me to check on chat-rooms to find out more about travelling in the US. That was a good idea.
4. Finally, she wanted me to write an e-mail to the lady at the travel agency and tell her that she'd been / she had been very unfriendly, and that we wouldn't come back. Alright, that's it then.

7 Modalverben in der indirekten Rede

1 a) David said (that) I had to feed Hunter his favorite food or he wouldn't eat it.
b) He said I should go for a walk with him twice a day.
c) He added that I could brush Hunter if I wanted to because he loved it.
d) He warned me that Hunter could get angry if I didn't pay attention to him from time to time.
e) David told me that I didn't have to let him sleep on the sofa.

2 a) Susan said I could jog with my dog every day, so I would be really fit.
b) But she added that I had to go for a walk with him twice a day…
c) She told me I could teach my dog some tricks and that would be funny.
d) She told me that I wasn't allowed to let him sleep in my bed.

3 a) Susan said I should take Carlos out of his cage every day.
b) She told me that Carlos wasn't allowed to eat sweets.
c) She said I had to clean his cage once a week.
d) She added that Carlos could bite me if I wasn't careful.
e) At the end she said that I was allowed to show him to her cousins if they wanted to see him.

8 Gemischte Aufgaben

1

direct speech	reported speech
1. "I may come back very late tonight."	c. *David:* "A girl in a dress said that she might come back very late that night."
2. "Can I have the keys to my room, please!"	f. *Annie:* "A drunk guy asked the receptionist to give him the keys to his room."
3. "Have you ever travelled alone?"	h. *Annie:* A girl with red hair asked someone whether she had ever travelled alone."
4. "I like long bus rides."	a. *David:* "A little boy told someone that he liked long bus rides."
5. "My parents will take me to Hawaii next summer."	e. *David:* "A young girl said her parents would take her to Hawaii the following summer."
6. "I spent last winter in Europe with my friends."	b. *Annie:* "An older traveller mentioned that he had spent the previous winter in Europe with his friends."
7. "When does the next bus to New York leave?"	d. *Annie:* "A backpacker asked his friend when the next bus to New York left."
8. "I'm going to stay in the cheapest hotel in Manhattan."	i. *David:* "Another very dirty-looking guy said that he was going to stay in the cheapest hotel in Manhattan."
9. "Don't tell my girlfriend that I went out late."	g. *David:* "A good-looking teenager told his friend not to tell his girlfriend that he had gone out late."

2 a)

next year	→	the following year
we	→	they
here	→	there
last week	→	the previous week
today	→	that day
now	→	then, at that time
I	→	he/she
this week	→	that week
you	→	I (Subjekt)/me (Objekt) / we (Subjekt)/me (Objekt)
my	→	his/hers
tomorrow	→	the following day
yesterday	→	the day before

3
a) Annie asked where we had stayed in Edinburgh.
b) She asked if/whether we had visited many museums.
c) She wanted to know where we had been before we had gone to Edinburgh.

4
a) *David:* "Are you going to go to the concert of Imagine Dragons with me, Carl?"
b) *Carl:* "I would love to go to this concert if you go there, too."
c) *David:* "Would your mom drive us to the concert, Carl? "
d) *Carl:* "Are we going to practice the guitar together in the holidays?"
e) *David:* "We'll improve our guitar skills a lot if we do this."
f) *Carl:* "We'll become famous rock stars if we continue practicing that much!"

5
a) My dad wanted to know what I had been doing that day while he had had to work.
b) He asked me if I had gone to my guitar lesson.
c) He asked me if I had been in the skater park.
d) He wanted to know if I had been hanging around with you the whole day.
e) My dad asked me when I had done my homework and if I had had any problems.
f) He even wanted to know why I hadn't prepared dinner yet.

6
a) A man in 1875 said that travelling by train was dangerous because trains were too fast.
b) Last year a friend of mine told me that he/she was afraid of travelling by plane, and that her/his cousin had died in a plane crash five years earlier.
c) One of my classmates said that his/her mother had gone to America by ship the year before and she had loved it.

d) My pen friend from Australia told me that he would fly to the moon as soon as possible because he/she hated life here/there. (Both are correct in this case – *here* = on Earth / *there* = in Australia)

e) My brother asked me whether I knew how bad it was for the environment that everybody was flying around the world all the time.

7 *Annie*:
Alright, here's what I found out: A guy called Jason wrote that we should definitely travel through Kansas. He said that he had lived there all his life and he thought it was great! Unfortunately he didn't tell us what was great. Well, then there was a girl called Anne. She warned us not to go to Chicago. She said that she hated it there and that she had moved there the year before. She explained that all we would see there would be cars.
Then there was Allison. She was in Mesa Verde, and wrote that it was the greatest place of all. They had arrived there the day before and she hoped that they would stay until the following Tuesday. That was when there would be a special guided tour of the Native American sites. That sounds good. And finally there was a note by a guy called Joey. He said that his sister had come back from her trip three days earlier and that she had been very excited about the Great Lakes. He thinks she was crazy because he had been there the winter before and it had been freezing cold.
So what do you think?

8 Möglicherweise hast du andere *einleitende Verben* gewählt. Das ist möglich und auch richtig solange du bedenkst, dass einige *reporting verbs* ein Objekt benötigen *(to tell sb, to ask sb)*.

1. *Annie:* Yes, – he told us that he had lost everything in the casino and asked us to give him some money.
2. *Carl:* Oh, yes. That was the girl in Death Valley. She said that her parents had forgotten her there, in the desert, and wondered if she could come with us.
3. *Annie:* She explained that she would stay and live there in that cave and promised us that we would understand why three years later.
4. *David:* Yes, he said that he would give us (the girls) a ride in his fantastic car but he also explained that he didn't take guys.
5. *Carl:* Yes, that was interesting. That was the priest in Colorado. He asked us whether we had thought about God and about our lives and mentioned that someone might ask us soon.
6. *Christoper:* Yes, how stupid. They explained we would find everlasting love if we kissed there.

9

1. Yesterday my father asked me where the pictures of his trip through America were.
2. I answered that I had not seen them.
3. Then he told me not to be stupid and added that he was sure he had had them the day before.
4. I told him that I really wasn't interested in his pictures.
5. Then Dad said that he always kept them in his cupboard, but they weren't there.
6. Luckily, my mother came and asked why he didn't take the ones right in front of him and leave me alone.
7. My dad said that that might be a good idea and thanked my mother.

Besser werden mit dem täglichen 10-Minuten-Training!

- Kleine Lernportionen: In 10 Minuten das Wichtigste draufhaben
- Mit vielen Übungen zu einem Schlüsselthema
- Leichte und schwere Übungen für mehr Lernerfolg

Englisch

Simple Present und Present Progressive
5. Klasse
ISBN 978-3-12-927389-0

Erste englische Texte schreiben
5./6. Klasse
ISBN 978-3-12-927518-4

Simple Past und Present Perfect
6./7. Klasse
ISBN 978-3-12-927392-0

If-Clauses
6.-8. Klasse
ISBN 978-3-12-927393-7

Direct Speech - Indirect Speech
7./8. Klasse
ISBN 978-3-12-927519-1

Deutsch

Diktate
5./6. Klasse
ISBN 978-3-12-927386-9

Texte schreiben
5./6. Klasse
ISBN 978-3-12-927388-3

Groß- und Kleinschreibung
5./6. Klasse
ISBN 978-3-12-927516-0

Wortarten
5./6. Klasse
ISBN 978-3-12-927517-7

Zeichensetzung
5.-7. Klasse
ISBN 978-3-12-927387-6

Mathematik

Textaufgaben
5. Klasse
ISBN 978-3-12-927527-6

Grundrechenarten
5. Klasse
ISBN 978-3-12-927394-4

Rechnen mit Brüchen
5./6. Klasse
ISBN 978-3-12-927395-1

Prozente und Zinsen
6.-8. Klasse
ISBN 978-3-12-927396-8

Rechnen mit Termen
7./8. Klasse
ISBN 978-3-12-927528-3

Diese und weitere Lernhilfen sind im Buchhandel erhältlich.
Weitere Informationen unter www.klett-lerntraining.de